Almost Ashore, Selected Poems

GERALD VIZENOR is Professor of American Studies at the University of New Mexico, and Professor Emeritus at the University of California, Berkeley. He is the author of more than twenty books on native histories, critical studies, and literature, including *The People Named the Chippewa: Narrative Histories*, and *Manifest Manners: Narratives on Postindian Survivance*.

Vizenor received the American Book Award for *Griever: An American Monkey King in China*, and a Distinguished Achievement Award from the Western Literature Association in 2005. His most recent books include *Fugitive Poses: Native American Indian Scenes of Absence and Presence*, two novels, *Chancers*, and *Hiroshima Bugi: Atomu 57*, two books of haiku, *Cranes Alight*, and *Raising the Moon Vines*, and a narrative poem, *Bear Island: The War at Sugar Point*.

He recently received an honorary degree, Doctor of Humane Letters, from Macalester College. Other honors include the Richard and Rhoda Goldman Distinguished Professor at the University of California, Berkeley; Literary Laureate, Honorary Literary Award from the San Francisco Public Library; and the Lifetime Literary Achievement Award, Native Writer's Circle of the Americas.

Vizenor is series editor of "American Indian Literature and Critical Studies" for the University of Oklahoma Press, and, with Diane Glancy, series editor of "Native Storiers: A Series of American Narratives" for the University of Nebraska Press.

Almost Ashore

SELECTED POEMS

GERALD VIZENOR

SALT

CAMBRIDGE

PUBLISHED BY SALT PUBLISHING
PO Box 937, Great Wilbraham. Cambridge PDO CB1 5JX United Kingdom
PO Box 202, Applecross, Western Australia 6153

© Gerald Vizenor, 2006

The right of Gerald Vizenor to be identified as the
author of this work has been asserted by him in accordance
with Section 77 of the Copyright, Designs and Patents Act 1988.

First published 2006

Printed and bound in the United Kingdom by Lightning Source

Typeset in Swift 9.5/13

ISBN-13 978 1 84471 271 7 paperback
ISBN-10 1 84471 271 0 paperback

TB

1 3 5 7 9 8 6 4 2

Contents

Crane Dancers

Almost Ashore

winter sea
over my shoes
shadows
and bright
round stones
at san gregorio

every wave
turns a season
forests adrift
empty shells
memory of fire
so faraway
in the mountains
and canyons

silent pools
raise my faces
by early tide
slight my hand
shoulders
almost ashore

light breaks
over the plovers
certain steps
my traces
blood, bone, stone
turn natural
and heavy waves
rush the sand

Crane Dance

honor me
once as a bear
touch me
by song

cover me
with bright leaves
october traces
by song

heavy snow
weighs the seasons
on my shoulders
by song

set me adrift
on the cold stones
at the shoreline
by song

raise me
in the white pine
and sumac
by song

leave me
near the moccasin
flower and birch
by song

teach me
the great dance
of sandhill cranes
by song

tease me
name the mongrels
sky eyes
by song

set me free
native liberty
twice a bear
by song

sandhill cranes
dragonflies
dance at sunrise
by song

Family Photograph

my father
clement vizenor
was a spruce
among the trees
a native
by totems

corded for pulp
by federal
indian agents
my father
turned away
from white earth
the reservation
colonial genealogies
and moved to the city
with family
at twenty three

native tricksters
teased his memory
shared dreams
and chance
in a mason jar
and ran low
across missions
stumps and stations
late at night
in wild stories

clement abided
the old men
dressed for war
cold and gray

once united
forever cursed
by uniforms

anishinaabe men
deserted twice
by name and praise
break memories
on the nicollet
island bridge
over the dark
mississippi river

arm bands adrift
on the water
wooden limbs
veterans
once civilized
by combat
and crusades
thrown back
forever
to evangelists
and charity

no indian agents
reservation masters
at the cold rails
on the bridge
counting allotments
forty acres short
only family photographs
washed ashore
in the city
that winter

no catechism
catholic catchwords
black lessons
promises of treaty
cash payments
for confirmations
and mercy lines
of racial shame

my father
was anishinaabe
an immigrant
in the city
painted ceilings
pure white
pasted wall paper
fancy flowers
for a union boss
and delivered
the first
white earth
native stories
in the suburbs

treaty women
naturals at the bar
heard my father
measure by promise
my blood at night

native stories
masterly
during the great
depression

inspired survivance
in unheated
cold water rooms
stained by kerosene
city blisters
memories in exile
and the fate
of families
burst overnight

clement vizenor
holds me
in a photograph
that winter
almost a smile
a new spruce

among the bricks
paint cans
half white earth
the other
native immigrant
moved to the city
and lost at cards

White Earth

october sunrise
shimmers in the birch
and cottonwoods

native tricksters
roam in the shadows
rearview mirrors
stories turn
back to stone
faces of shamans
and ravens
on the federal roads

colonial missions
plunder white pine
torture the crane
close cultures
native ceremonies
for the season

government agents
hunker over the ruins
underestimate
the woodland dead
in leather bound
ledger books

benedictory beads
crucifixions
rage over night
twice renounced
in the reeds
meadow larks
old healers

poisoned
by sacraments
on the wing

timber cruisers
muted roses
hues at pine point
count canoes
manners of silence
over wild rice

black lace
purled by children
at saint benedict
catholic schools
archaic ruse
that covets
land and trees
native liberty
general allotments
winter graves
stony survivance
among the bloody
stumps of white pine

cathedrals
of the winter nights
crack the ice
and curse
shaman cures
at the shoreline
centerfolds
tricky stories
medicine bundles

once marooned
by soldiers
await the fire
in great museums

bright moon
breaks on the bridge
stone faces
catch the light
native warriors
slowly cross
the lonesome city

white earth
shadows on a bus
last forever
in late movies
missionaries
stain their bodies
at the altars

native storiers
tease the cruisers
black bears
northern lights
and turn seasons
forever at the source
of lake itasca

jesuit dominion
ghostly crossbones
over birds
beaver and muskrat
trade pelts

by treaty fashion
felt hats
and eagle feathers
decorate the rush
at the greedy
end of enlightenment
and civilization

moose browse
near the mission ruins
abandoned stations
of the cross
and toilet doors
undone by storms

mundane litanies
caught by shamans
in the weeds
and touchwood
alight twice
in the holy seams

mighty ravens
inspire nicknames
dead men
black beads
at night
by visions
and trickery
and return
to their embassies
in the white pine

Distance

my father
turned again
last night
to hear
native exiles
over the silence
of his unmarked
city grave
at so great
a family distance

closer by rain
shadows
at the treeline
cut across
a lonesome
native scene

bright sunrise
two ravens
bounce
on the birch
crowns
and break
the unbearable
stories of his death

Guthrie Theater

american indian
outside the guthrie
forever wounded
by tributes
high western
movie mockery
decorations
invented names
trade beads
federal contracts
limps past
the new theater

wounded indian
comes to attention
on a plastic leg
and delivers
a smart salute
with the wrong hand

precious children
muster nearby
theatrical poses
under purple
tapestries
castles
and barricades
on stage
with reservation plans

native overscreams
rehearsed
on stage
at sand creek

blaze of bodies
at mystic river
frozen ghost dancers
chased to death
by the seventh cavalry
at wounded knee

culture wars
wound the heart
and dishonor
the uniform
forsaken warriors
retire overnight
in cardboard suites
under the interstates

american indian
decorated for bravery
invented names
salutes the actors
with the wrong hand
at the guthrie

treaties break
behind the scenes
night after night
the actors
new posers
mount and ride
on perfect ponies
out to the wild
cultural westerns
hilly suburbs
with buffalo bill

Raising the Flag

native woman
once a healer
by a thousand years
anishinaabe time
shivered alone
in a telephone booth
at the corner
of tenth and chicago
in minneapolis

she learned english
in federal schools
a cold place
for sacred names
and was outed
on a farm
milking cows
for another race

federal agents
landed in heavy
leather coats
promised education
by native
separation
and cultural
dominance
at a cruel distance

she wore summer
jumble clothes
patent red
charity shoes
cracked

by winter
and warmed
her cold fingers
by breath
checked twice
the coin return

city soldiers
poured grain belt
draft beer
shouted squaw
teased her grave
native stories
woodland shine
and secrets

drunken soldiers
cursed the memory
of native warriors
woodland shamans
mauled her breasts
for the cavalry

she was down
with a sacred name
alone forever
in a telephone booth
unbearable marks
of civilization
waiting to hear
the voices
of her children
stolen by welfare
security agents

she turned
at the winter bar
raised a flag
of eagle feathers
and honored
by song
hole in the day
pillager warriors
at bear island
and sugar point

Shaman Breaks

timber barons
unearthed a fortune
by white pine
and cursed
the old stone shaman
over the breaks

moths beat
night after night
at the cold
window panes
unaware
the faint light
not a day

leaves abide
the season
mighty splendor
and ravens
smarten the birch
and maples

fur traders
bought the beaver
fox and otter
overturned
river shores
and wild rice

blue soldiers
hunted the moose
and bears
young pillagers
and lost the war
at leech lake

native stories
arise with the cranes
moccasin flowers
and the old shamans
over the breaks

new tourists
haunt the ruins
and mimic
the old stone shaman
over the breaks

nasturtiums
decorate
the barbed wire
fences down
to the dead river

mercy stones
out of reach
by traces
of the moon
ordinary
native stories
fall apart
overnight

Crow Stories

three crows
blue in the bright
winter sun
trickster poses
in the birch

bloody sumac
buried overnight
in the hard
crusted snow

deer crack
the bony crests
treacherous
river ice

crow stories
tease memories
cruel seasons
of rusted plows
barbed wire
and lonesome
timber traders
at city docks
suddenly
out of breath

Winter Camp

night tribes
tease the morning
and chase
water witches
in the marsh
by ritual thunder
pitch and scent
of wild flowers
mowed weeds
on the road

thunder storms
shroud the otter
signatures
on the river

freight trains
and moths
break the light
native stories
and fluorescence
over rose
and cedar street

blue lights
ancient stones
shattered
on the southern
pacific tracks
far from home

Mission Road

kingfisher
waits on the wire
over the dusty
mission road
north of brainerd

aspen leaves
brighten
at night
in the cold
autumn rain

sounds turn
by chance
seasons
at the treeline

rivers darken
and slow
the motion
of winter clouds
sandhill cranes
return
and dance
across a meadow
near leech lake

Blue Horses

painted horses
prison riders
by morning
blue in the canyons
green and brown
western posts
forever mounted
in ledger art

migrant traders
wait in silence
common wares
tin and china
by manners
parasols
and chintz
resistance
fades the colors

prison riders
crowned
by museums
old world
curators
envy the race
primitive art
and native liberty

ledger mounts
blue horses
ride again
with franz marc
chagall
kandinsky
and quick to see

Hand Prints

think about hands
and eyes
spider webs
charms
birch bark
four directions
winter count
figures
eagle feathers
circles of the sun
and heart
bear claws
hand prints
on stone
pictomyths
woodland tricksters
silent ravens
balanced
in the white pine

Window Ice

native storiers
by chance
and ruse
untrace
my seasons
certainties
curses
run thin
as shadows
and silence
in early light

window ice
clouds creased
faces change
heart and stone
mother
father
winter bears
on the cold
window
reach out
and touch
memories
other families
hunters
of blood
and stone

light holds
origins
cut of seasons
bright blue
meadows

bony scraps
survivance
by tides
and wild rivers

native storiers
by tease
create color
nicknames
thieves of fires
animals
water birds
sough of voices
circle of footprints
in the snow

Certainties

certainties
cultures
blood quanta
cursed
wounded
stories
by surnames
spring clouds
run thin
overnight

a father
turns bear
at night
touched
and teased
in other worlds
forever
by chance

stolen light
in the cold
murky
river water
brightens
the otter
shadows
creased
by seasons
thunder
winter cuts
stories ashore
of faces
in the stone

Praise Ravens

seven ravens
praise the winter
and tease
the distance
of shamans
at white earth

pale poplar
crowned by snow
sumac horns
abandoned cars
half buried
at the roadside

native meadows
marked by treaties
fox runs
beaver dams
undone
by rusted plows
birch stations
of the cross

snowmobiles
bay overnight
city savages
rush the crests
and snare
their necks
on barbed wire

seven ravens
bounce in the poplar
a winter dance
over spent cultures
dead in the weeds

Bear Walkers

twice touched
by fire
overnight
creation
white pine
bears
at the heart
stories of wild
seasons
and folds
of summer light

Haiku Scenes

March Moon

march moon
shimmers on the concrete
snail crossing

clumsy bees
circle the wisteria
room by room

trumpet vines
ride the arbor in a storm
umbrellas flare

Safe Harbor

rain shadows
children share umbrellas
late school bus

moths at dusk
flutter in the porch lantern
safe harbor

october leaves
tumble down the sidewalk
dogs on a leash

Trumpeter Swans

three sparrows
bounce in the red tulips
sunday picnic

windy night
acacia brightens the bench
early service

trumpeter swans
circle bad medicine lake
silently

Crow Dance

leech lake storm
two plovers run with the waves
natural beat

sunday morning
three children in white shoes
geese on the water

prairie clothes lines
children dance in the shadows
encore in the sheets

Trumpet Vines

black butterflies
dance in the dandelions
double time

trumpet vines
high in the ancient oak
children on swings

sunflowers
bow in a heavy rain
city bus stop

Canyon Road

march wisteria
brightens the iron fence
juncos on the wire

windy morning
boughs of the old chestnut tree
heave the magpies

canyon road
party in the sculpture garden
dancing elephants

Picnic Bench

plum blossoms
down after a heavy rain
faces in the pool

winter rain
elephant leaves turn to listen
stories at the fence

picnic bench
sparrows gather for lunch
cold wind

Magnolias

winter rain
magnolias lose their bright
faces overnight

golden apples
children prance around the tree
heavy rain

sunday morning
an old man in white shoes
mongrel on a leash

Natural Balance

march snow
blue shadows in the park
circle of footprints

gray morning
only a spring daffodil
hides the winter

strong wind
cardinals catch the red berries
natural balance

Snow Crowns

crowns of snow
decorate the pinyon boughs
overnight reign

foggy morning
squirrels in the eucalyptus
cones resound

bright nasturtiums
cover the abandoned bus
faces of children

Mountain Snow

mountain snow
squirrels rush the apricots
late apologies

aspen shiver
winter storm in the mountains
crows on a lawn chair

catalpa blossoms
decorate the wet black bench
nowhere to sit

Square Dance

pinyon boughs
reach over the portal
voices in a storm

sudden thaw
children chase pencil boats
late for school

fat green flies
square dance across the grapefruit
honor your partner

Fancy Dance

storm clouds
lake waves crash on the shoreline
crows sway in the birch

broken pencils
float away in the river
distant school bell

wooden clothespins
fancy dance on the line
thunderstorm

Natural Duty

Choir of Memory

grave faces
of the late
window gods
appease
my shadow
and break
the fierce silence
overnight
by memory
of cruel cities

perfect names
aryan chauffeurs
at the reich
mileposts
in the dark
firestorms
erased
entire families
outrun
on the rails

old storiers
cloak the shame
creation turns
and rage
against misery
black mercy
footmen
in the lounge
mockery
by chance
or godsend
on the night train

antwerp
to amsterdam

ceremony
and memory
tormented
by the stations
break of light

my shouts
slight tributes
sentiments
of resistance
almost lost
on the cloudy
cold coasts
of the second
world war

blue portraits
dark eyes
weary children
forsaken
by the seasons
winter coats

silent nations
rush past
the meadows
festivals
mitzva
secular unions

sole relatives
reflected
night after night
on the dirty
train windows
vanish in the light
at the stations

family traces
beholden
and imagined
on the glass
by a jeweler
in a mighty choir
of memory
forever
in motion
on the train
to amsterdam

Paul Celan

slow death
of images
cities
seasons
at war

the unbearable
clear sky
sudden storms
of memory
thunderous
breaks
of lightning
that linger
in the eye

summer tease

fire trace

stone sorrow

black memory
no rescues
by irony
praise
over silence
at the wall

the wild
restrained
by time
and copies
of winter

unwary
untaught
in stories
near the end

the pleasure
of masks
two scenes
and wing
nothing
is ever lost
at night

ruby throated
hummingbirds
inspire children
to survive
one more
memorable
afternoon
by flowers

brown ants
haunt an old man
bodies towed
brothers
the ashes
of entire
ancient families
across a continent
on the portal

heavy snow
without a voice

covers the city
in whispers
rumors of silence
trace of poetry
by morning
a mighty reign
over the parapets
and pinyon
boughs

black gates
of paris
disguised by snow
fake shame
not our fate
a patient
show of hands

snow mounds
touch and shape
the doors
by memory

empty rooms

music in the beams

death in a key

that lonesome
turn of eyes
at the door
the only
sovereignty

paul celan
inspires
our resistance
by state
and portrait
extremes
in the river
dark and cold

Huffy Henry

john berryman
spilled gin
twice that night
by his hoary
party laughter

the poet grazed
through the summer
garden chairs
hunchvoiced henry
over centuries
of manners
and lusty sighs

soiree women
twice bound
in seersucker
polyester lace
parse their names
out of time
from the bushes

trace of seasons
on the run
resurrections
rage of literacy
routs of fancy
eternal cues
promises of light
by the academy

henry grins
always
a great poet

and word runner
tormented
by the ironies
of tower hill

kittens wheeze
every night
continents away
by telephone

henry is roused
by the voices
the flight
and squabbles
of sparrows
over picnic poems

river mosquitoes
and pretenders
marooned
that humid
summer night
on his sacred
blood and irony

huffy henry
stumbles
in the playground
after dark
and blue
children
forever
at his side
count the strokes
of empty swings

September Light

pearl returns
alone and scared
from the clinic
shadows gather
plum hues
beneath her eyes

she opens
closes
closet doors
tells the plants
one by one
she is dying

pearl burns
seven love letters
from a felon
counts shares
passions
travel time
unhappy diary days

turns her clothes
sleeve by sleeve
across the seasons
next year

pearl unhooks
the hooks
unties the ties
undresses
for the garden

cosmos the cat
shiny black
inspects the sleeves
wary of moves

in the tender
september light
she raises
her breasts
hand to hand
in flight

pearl circles
with the birds
blue silence
turns suddenly
on empty
trees at dusk
and crashes
through the glass

Medicine Hat

morning rain
wind traces
on the windows
downtown
at the queen's
hotel in moosomin

wispy clouds
rush low
over the fences
unpainted
on the road
to regina

swift current
blue flowers
arise in a patch
of sunlight

jacob werner
waves a white hose
over his garden
cabbages
eternal
immigrant
at home
in medicine hat

strangers
admire his vegetables
sunflowers
bright lettuce
rhubarb
and he mentions

by name
each of his wives

french canadians
raised chins
shadows
by the green
course to the barn

pillars of dust
stanchions
prairie winds
out back
in the cities

catholic spires
arise in the distance
over the bright
fields of mustard

a waitress
combs her long
blond hair
over her forehead
covers a red boil
and smiles

tender fern
hides the mushrooms
faces hidden
on the trail

cumulus clouds
tow the thunder

lightning cracks
over saskatchewan

three white shirts
clap together
on a windy
summer porch

sunlight bounces
on the river
breaks
over the marsh
blackbirds
meadow larks
alight in the reeds

cattle browse
under the lazy
oil wells

a school bus
unfurls a prairie
standard
of orange dust
cuts the fields
into movable
homesteads

mountains
blue and green
float away
in the distance
noisy streams
tease the salmon

arm at dawn
near kamloops

cache creek
children
and farm birds
in flight
at the water main
sprinklers
at dusk

black bears
stand in cedar
shadows
on the rise
by the moon

bright lights
of the city
shimmer
at the base
of the mountains
houses turn
by rows
overnight
eyes of animals
wary creases
at the treelines

North Dakota

east

the whole moon
burns behind jamestown

seven wings of geese
light the thin ice

west

the asian sun
bloody on the interstate

spring flowers
break on the gray prairie

exit

fingerprints
on the rearview mirror

feral shadows
transposed near fargo

Tyranny of Moths

feathery moths
flutter on the screen
unbearable
sounds of summer

oblivious tonight
that my reading light
is not my day

stout bodies
cut and bounce
near a crack
in the screen
and beat inside
a paper shade
sacraments
of a monumental
natural presence

we are drawn
forever
by the moths
to other lights
neighbors
down the road

Grassy Attic

sunday rain
black sun
bruised hues
on the meadows
grassy
blue attic
coloring book

green horizon
bright folds
over the scarlet
houseflies
rosy sparrows

silhouettes
painted twice
buried red
floats across
shadows
solemn faces
sun creased
browse
in the rich
purple
buffalo grass

marble feathers
catch the
last rainbows
on the window

solemn scenes
unmoored
at the corner

cold blues
cue and promise
crash by turns

frogs leap
over the blue table
and crash
on the surface
of an orange pond

magic trains
climb the bright
paper birch
fantastic animals
break the leash
in the winter
window mirrors

Camp Grounds

righteous armies
of abraham
mighty jesus
brothers
by his name
one god
betray the birch
white pine
beaver dams
native memory

summer sorties
near the precious
tourist triangle
walker
park rapids
bemidji
fabricated
aluminum lures
mission lace
plastic flowers
decorate
gruesome traces
of disease
and the fur trade

blue butterflies
small birds
slow insects
dead on radiators
and windshields
of massive
vacation vans

giant animals
cut whistle grass
slowly at night
in this place

woodland rivers
rise black
and dammed
on reservations
the trees
endure
on postcards

native ghosts
torment campers
night swimmers
wave lights
and return
to the manger
with stories
of demons
in the dead water

Dead Rivers

mississippi river
died without notice
at the university
plastic flowers
decorate the gloomy
concrete atriums

carp yawn
and wash ashore
at dawn

acid rain
disfigures faces
birch and marrow
common scenes
shrouded
by fine umbrellas

thick water
storms in the sewers
slander and lust
downriver
city overnight

native memories
familiar traces
float away
brightly
out of reach

shadows arise
near shore
shiver and cross
black beams
in the dead river

Berkeley Storm

hazy morning
hides the towers
cold rituals
under breath

silent warriors
mark the tracks
dead routes
railroad sighs
on the southern
pacific siding

family stories
secured
by couplers
weary humor
abandoned
in depot graves

windigo faces
blue traces
on the concrete
at spruce
and cedar streets

headlights
burn in the haze
white moths
shriven
beat outside
the stained
rose window
rainbows
in a winter storm

Columbus Endures

columbus endures
as an old lady
in the park
she wears robes
and smells
woolly
of moth balls
and gum

columbus endures
as an old lady
she trudges
in a heavy
winter coat
and waits
on a park bench
for the snow

columbus endures
as an old lady
she pulls
a threadbare
blanket
over her mouth
and shouts
landfall ahead
on the green

columbus endures
as an old lady
she dreams
by day
of an opera
orchestra

mounted
out of tune
on appaloosas

columbus endures
as an old lady
she draws
bathwater
for the return
by irony
and chance
to the old world

Tricky Auras

remember
the trick routes
homeward
bound tonight

noise weary
on the interstates

trucks brake
across our families
conceptions
common corners

governments
overdone
by race
malice
raze stories
native presence
otter poses
and memory

houses undone
graves aside
trees deposed
by dominion
in perfect flower

summer faces
generations
and silhouettes
by seasons
forever separated
at the door

new cultures
change the shadows
stain the rivers

city sunrise
over the concrete
thresholds
broken
by weeds
windows
in utter ruins

tricky auras
shimmer
on the barriers
out of time
and irony
in the wild
morning light

Creation Fires

thunderstorms
prey on the prairie
families at night

warriors of the bear
crash through the screen
summer faces

chapel shadows
faint at the corners
stone and bone

dreary shamans
hunker in the rainy
cottonwoods

cracked windows
scatter the rainbows
creation fires

Museum Bound

thunderclouds
fold nations
native words
stone traces
summer solstice
out of place

whale oil
pianos
commerce
by rivers
meadows
blue pemmican
beaver hats
bright wispy
moccasin flowers
traded
for laudanum

mission windows
and mirrors
double overnight
native shadows
crease the naves

new testaments
of the concrete
fast foods
dead and lonely
at stations
of the cross

black squirrels
depot bears
carrion crows
march at the treeline
dead visions
coin returns
and ethnic
slot machines

willows bow
in the heavy rain
noisy cultures
out of time
clutter the names
of every animal
and bird
museum bound

Mission Motel

famous animals
spoke here
and birds
celebrated
this native place
centuries
of white pine
downed
by cruisers
and missions
before the neon
vacancy sign
sculptured carpets
polymer furniture
flocked interiors
motel red
and bloody
handprints
at the bar

windigoo stories
return at night
by thunder
and crow
trickster scenes
in the plastic
paper birch

dusty atrium
corporate colonists
gather for lunch
china made
in pure
resin shirts

fluorescence
pale and empty
heartbeats
censured
in aluminum chairs

missions cut
around the green
indoor pool
seasoned forever
by chlorine

manifest moteliers
voted early
one bright summer
around the world
to block the sun
protect the carpets
painted orchards
fruity scenes
on the gray
cracked concrete

War Games

return alone
shadows
of the cold wars
that afternoon
at the corner
drugstore

outback
at the loading dock
our surnames
weathered
by storms
on the rough
red bricks

heroic scenes
weakened
on the inside
sun and urine
bullet holes
on the outside

saturday night
corner warriors
black and red
at the end
twice dead
by firing squads

surnames
scored on bricks
nickish
maag
quinn

anderson
petesch
renner
bold soldiers

last words
for school girls
the dancers
and mourners
praise war
over the irony
and practice
of death

returned alone
to the drugstore
that afternoon
counted wounds
familiar scenes
bullet holes
on the red bricks
our showy names
stand forever

Surrender

the longest war
ended at dusk
last summer
by surrender
behind the tonics
and hand cream

my friends
waited outback
and declared
the loading dock
a homeland
drug store
and promised
the world
native liberty

my enemies
touched by women
always survive
no one ever died
at the counter

my relatives
tease the prisoners
count wounds
masks of torture
every winter
and change
nicknames
by the seasons

Museum Flies

october morning
two black flies
converse
over the cold
marble thighs
at the museum

two black flies
circle wide
the gray
stone heads
land on mine

waved away
to another head
the flies widen
their cut
sensuous curves
nose to penis
cold thigh
shoulder
warm body

black flies
pose on the sunny
warriors
and clowns
in magical flight
across the nudes
stone faces
black uniforms

museum guards
bound in linen
bear arms
fly swatters
memorable stunts
mighty flies
museum marbles

Depot Graves

manservants
turn wary
on the last trains
north to milwaukee
sweet mary
through the junk

the old men
carry brass keys
low censers
locking toilets
at the depot graves

angles of sun
glance and break
over the dead
milk trucks
warehouses
oil weeds
derailed boxcars
stenciled
for repairs

the founders
plainly disguised
in creased
morning coats
at the crossings
glance back
in photographs
once giants
now ashore
in dead water

Out of Order

crows on the wire
whole moons
bounce back
on the wet black
mission road
north of white earth

birch leaves
shudder
near the cold
windy
lakeshore
of bad medicine

engines moan
surrender
to the haze
that october
morning
near beaulieu
cities declared
out of order
for the season

Double Negatives

my son is away
overnight
at clear lake
with grandparents

three times
his age
alone after dark
memories
keep me awake

ordinary dreams
over praised
first places
where we learned
to swim
river and dock

beached poems
file folders
candles
dead pens
on my desk

new words
old faces
in the audience
that night

english teachers
overlooked
past sentences
agreement
double negatives
invited me to read
imagistic poems

Sandprints

ocean beats
my heart
stories
word by word
in the sand
erased
on the waves

museums
court names
money
manners
and erase
impermanence
by stone
encomium
only waves
of irony
survive
the posers

sandprints
names
memories
traces of animals
cowries
crane totem
retouched
after the storm

Rural Routes

vanity marks
the spring
blossoms
elusive words
for seniors
at the cracked
white marble
prescription
counter

touch the face
of wild children
disguised fancy
for books
and crowns
noisy beggars
bruised forever
by evolution
cold fast food
red candy

mail carriers
bear the last traces
of winter
near home
seed catalogues
newspapers
time out
broken
by the weather
that morning
on a rural route

Trickster Cats

trickster cats
rush the fence
in silence
and roam
on the black
stained
church windows

umbrellas twist
by services
gospel cues
native stories
one early
spring morning

ice boats
crease the waves
and shimmer
downhill
in a parade

a heroic
red spider
climbs the map
alpine trails
over mountains
in minutes

trickster cats
haunt the parish
sanctuary
nose the cold
nostalgic wind
at the rail

Crow Nests

crows return
by words
bold messages
perched high
in the october
white pine

crows strut
on country roads
parapets
cemetery stones
past the dead
homesteads

crows preen
feathers clean
cold rain
brightens
precious stones
stolen beads

Shirley by Winter

gray snow
crusted
at the corner
time to change
february
every season
she said
transforms
memories
of her father

shirley abandons
men by winter
bony feet
in a white mirror
and turns
abstract sorrows
wild colors
on a canvas

shirley deserted
the house
by spring
ancient dust
returned
to the carpets
cloth walls
and catholic boys

static electricity
torments
the calico cat
stair by stair
unfinished studio

barely painted
canvases
stacked in rows

shirley waits
over cigarettes
at the cold
yellow window
and wanders
at night
over glaciers
deserts
and touches
that elusive light
in the eyes
of rabbits
sleeve dogs
and old men

Treuer Pond

treuer pond
shimmers
by late summer
lily pads
canoe adrift
silent tease
of catchwords
surnames
from libra cusps
as the wind
pitched
the cattails
redwing blackbirds
turn the sun
at the shoreline

pond promises
migration
canada geese
blue herons
mudheads
birds unnamed
never owned
by homesteaders
or their heirs
almost lost
at treaty games
metes and bounds
to natives
and the state

names ashore
kingfishers
crash in the water
ancient dancers
raise their hands
and sing
in the tidy barn

Homewood Hospital

noisy sparrows
at the great
window box
every morning
commercial
shock therapy

the orderlies
secure by turns
the chains
of memory
bear the mark
of cain
she said
bear the mark
of abel
she said
bear the mark
of everyone
she said
braced again
for medical mercy

heavy snow
in the city
seasons
miscarried
she said
listen to stories
of disunion
geiger counters
dead birds
at the window
she said
and the literature
of violence
shock therapy

Blue Bottle

the old woman
so happy
to meet a friend
in the garden
raised her dress
high above
her skinny legs
to wipe tears

she touched
a secret note
to a lover
twice sealed
in a blue bottle
floated back
to the garden

Silhouettes

october storm
leaves shiver
ants cross
at the window
brown rows
against
a cold wind

a child
waits inside
at the sill
blows clouds
over scenes
and teases
the ants
by seasons
and silhouettes

Gentle Pain

gentle pain
magnolias
in the snow
children
chase
a white dog
on the hill
bright twigs
run the icy
spring rivers
toward home
everything
ordinary
but the pain

Paper Plane

october storm
delivered
the skeleton
of a kite
that crash
landed
last week
in a giant maple
at the park

children
waited in slick
red coats
all morning
under
the boughs
bright leaves
break free

Whole Moon

north dakota
wavers
on the horizon
at dusk
as the whole
moon rises
over jamestown

seven flights
of canada geese
break the blue
cold water
at the heart
of a prairie lake

finger prints
mark the rearview
mirror
as the eyes
of asian gods
glance back
in a night sky

City Crumbs

noisy sparrows
under a faded
john deere sign

stout vines
hold the cracked
bricks together

no window
feeders to haunt
by morning

tractor sparrows
pounce and capture
crumbs on the run

broken bearclaws
bits of scones
stone by stone

First Leaves

april morning
sunlight breaks
on the birch
bare shadows
of first leaves
cover my hands

spring flowers
elusive petals
open and close
juncos bounce
on my face
vanish in a name

Cat Parade

two cats
inside the curtain
one parades
and the other
composed
paws crossed
at the window

mourning doves
sough nearby
on the fence
trade songs
natural sounds
presence
and caution

gentle sunrise
that morning
after an overnight
thunderstorm

two cats
reverse their moves
clean claws
and catch
by chatter
image and eye
tricky house
sparrows
and other birds
on the glass

Tropisms

woodpeckers
hammer by rows
at dawn
five
seven
five
hemlock
haiku holes

Natural Duty

high blues
flower in the spring
a natural duty
of hummingbirds
already conceals
a black cat

every shadow
an eternal tease
of the sun
warm wind
perfect scent
of creation
magical flight

the weary cat
silent pose
stiffens
wide of the blues
until dark
a natural duty

Printed in the United States
57755LVS00002B/55-159